Book 3 in the Land to Lots™ Trilogy

COUNTING YOUR FORTUNE

MANAGING YOUR BIGGER FUTURE

A STEP-BY-STEP GUIDE FOR LEVERAGING THE LAUNCH SEQUENCE®
IN YOUR NEXT MASTER PLANNED COMMUNITY

Other Books by Carter Froelich

Land to Lots: How to Borrow Money You Don't Have to Pay Back and LAUNCH Master Planned Communities

Fields to Fortune: Planning Your Bigger Future

Activating Your Fortune: Implementing Your Bigger Future

Book 3 in the Land to Lots® Trilogy

COUNTING YOUR FORTUNE

MANAGING YOUR BIGGER FUTURE

A STEP-BY-STEP GUIDE FOR LEVERAGING THE LAUNCH SEQUENCE® IN YOUR NEXT MASTER PLANNED COMMUNITY

CARTER FROELICH

ethos
collective

Published by Igniting Souls
PO Box 43, Powell, OH 43065
IgnitingSouls.com

LCCN: 2025910227
Paperback ISBN: 978-1-63680-520-7
Hardback ISBN:978-1-63680-521-4
Ebook ISBN: 978-1-63680-522-1

Available in paperback, hardcover, e-book, and audiobook.

Table of Contents

Part 3: Maintain

Scan the QR Code below to Access
Supplemental Documents and
Book Bonuses

Introduction

Welcome to the third and final installment of the Land to Lots® Trilogy, a value enhancement series with all the information you need to take your master planned community from start to finish. By reading this book, you are completing a journey from land to lots and from fields to fortune. As your guide on this journey, I offer you the expertise of over forty years of helping people like you achieve their land development goals. My team at Launch Development Finance Advisors works with land developers, commercial developers, and home builders to finance their infrastructure using a proven process called The Launch Sequence®. Before we dive in, let's review the Launch Sequence process as a whole and assess how far we have already come.

What is The Launch Sequence®?

The Launch Sequence is a unique process we at Launch Development Finance Advisors have developed by working with land developers and home builders around the United States for over forty years. In assisting them with finance and public infrastructure through a myriad of different means, we have perfected our processes and created an infinitely applicable land development value-enhancement process that assists our clients in financing public infrastructure with long-term (twenty-five-plus-year) non-recourse, tax-exempt bonds, reducing costs, and mitigating risks, all with the goal of enhancing project profitability and returns.

The genius of The Launch Sequence is it enables our clients to borrow money to finance infrastructure in such a way that the end users of the project pay it back. In essence, you get to borrow money you don't have to repay.

It almost sounds too good to be true, doesn't it?

But the truth is, The Launch Sequence works every time, all the time. It works on big projects. It works on small projects. It works in every state and every situation. The Launch Sequence is a flexible formula, but it is also a living process, and both factors contribute to its enduring success.

Every time we have a "learning experience," whether good or bad, we incorporate it into The Launch Sequence. We use several tools to memorialize and universalize our experiences, but regardless of the situation, we learn and grow from each of our thousands of transactions so our clients can benefit.

So, how does it work? Fundamentally, every developer starts with a jigsaw puzzle box. Inside are their goals, challenges, and opportunities, but they are all puzzle pieces jumbled together. We take that box and dump it out on the table. From there, it's just a matter of sorting the puzzle pieces by color, shape, and image as we get a feel for the size and possibility of the project. In other words, we find out where the client wants to go and what tools we have at our disposal based on the specific state and jurisdiction to help our client complete their vision.

The Launch Sequence has three stages: the Planning Process, the Implementation Process, and the Management Process. *Fields to Fortune: Planning Your Bigger Future* is the first book in this series, and it covers the Planning Process in detail. Next is *Activating Your Fortune: Implementing Your Bigger Future*, which explains the Implementation Process. If you haven't read either of these, I highly recommend picking them up first. It gives you every tool necessary to formulate an adaptive project plan. This book turns to the Management Process, where we take the plans we've implemented and develop long-term strategies for managing the project. Now is the time to take your land development project from ideas to reality.

Why Should I Care?

The alternative to The Launch Sequence is simply hiring an underwriter to do your Special District (e.g., CFD, CDD, Metro, MUD, SID, PID, etc.) bond sizing and be done with it. I mentioned this in the first two books, and I will repeat it here: I have great admiration and affection for my underwriting colleagues. There is no question that they are very good at what they do.

It is important to remember, however, that underwriters don't work for you. Yes, the underwriters are the ones who issue the bonds and secure the money, and ultimately, that is the goal of any type of Special District financing. Nonetheless, the two perspectives differ in that the underwriters typically work first for the bond buyers, then for the district or jurisdiction, and only lastly for the developer. They will necessarily see things from the perspective of issuing the largest bond possible (as they are paid based upon the par amount of the bonds) and of doing so in the shortest time possible, with a bond structure that allows them the easiest and fastest marketing and sales period.

As such, these goals can and do often ignore the realities of:

- Developing a master planned community
- Changing real estate market conditions
- Total effective property tax rate considerations
- Construction phasing
- Development impact fee credits
- Other benefiting land owners
- Oversizing requirements
- Other reimbursement mechanisms
- The developer's Project Vision™
- The Return Factor Question™
- Financing goals
- Business plan

Since I began providing professional advisory services to the private sector in the mid-1980s, I have had one driving interest—that of my private sector developer clients. Neither I nor the Launch Development Financing Advisor (Launch) professionals work for underwriters, financial advisors, districts, or the public sector. Our only focus is on helping our private sector development clients achieve their vision and business plan. When we implement The Launch Sequence, we genuinely want the best for our clients.

Underwriters and financial advisors rarely have the experience we do when working across the entirety of a project. We first and foremost consider what our clients want to achieve and how they will judge their financial success. We then lay out detailed plans to achieve these goals. We take a much broader view of what we can do for our clients to help them finance infrastructure, reduce costs, and mitigate risks, all with the goal of enhancing project profitability.

Throughout this exposition of the Management Process, you will see many lists of questions. Use these as a guide to start personalizing The Launch Sequence to your unique needs. We can provide structure and a method, but nothing will take flight until the details of *your* project are on the launch pad.

PART 1

Monitor

This Isn't the End

Even though this book deals with the last stage of the Launch Sequence, this does not conclude your master planned community project. Why not? Because the Management Process is all about taking everything you've built in the Planning Process and the Implementation Process and ensuring it will last for years to come. Once your project has been planned and implemented, the most lengthy process of the three—management—can begin.

Before we start to look at what the Management Process involves, let's review the Launch Sequence from the beginning. In the Planning Process, we begin by taking our clients through an interview where they explain their Project Vision in as much detail as possible. We then conduct a version of Dan Sullivan's D.O.S. Conversation® from the Strategic Coach® Program. D.O.S. stands for Dangers, Opportunities, and Strengths. By organizing project information into these categories for our client, we can make sure our client's potential roadblocks can be overcome, their opportunities captured, and their project and company advantages leveraged.

During the Planning Phase, we also have our clients answer the Return Factor Question, which identifies the financial metric they prefer to use to judge their financial performance. Are they driven by the internal rate of return (IRR) or by nominal dollars (e.g., multiple)? Most of our clients say they want both; however, we ask that they only select one response because the answer to this question will set the stage for the selection of the financing vehicle(s) to be used in the project financing and inform us as to what will need to be included in legal agreements with the jurisdiction, agencies, and Special Districts.

If you have just finished reading *Fields to Fortune* and *Activating Your Fortune,* all of this is going to sound very familiar. But I can't emphasize enough the importance of Project Vision, the D.O.S. Conversation, and the Return Factor Question. The response to these questions is where the financial destination of the Project is laid out. Without this destination in mind, we cannot implement or manage anything with efficiency because we lack clarity from the very beginning.

With our newfound clarity, we begin to handcraft the detailed Project Path and Plan™ for our client. The Project Path and Plan is the blueprint document we prepare that enumerates all of the financing vehicles we want to include in our project financing, as well as all of the specific deal points we will need to include in the entitlement or financing agreements that will be in place during the duration of the project's buildout.

This document is curated to the specific needs of the client based on their goals and objectives. It is handcrafted to ensure it will provide certainty as to what financing tools will be available during the buildout of the project, but will also create flexibility for the client to be able to adapt to changes in the local real estate market.

The high-level concepts contained within the Project Path and Plan are then simplified and included in The Launch Finance Plan, which is presented to the decision makers (e.g., jurisdictional councils and staff) for their consideration and feedback. The presentation of the Finance Plan and the responses from the jurisdictional representatives provide the client with clarity on what the jurisdiction is willing to assist with as part of the financing, what they will not do, and what they may request in return.

With this real-time feedback from the jurisdictional representatives, we generally know with approximately eighty percent certainty the elements of the Finance Plan we can count on. We can determine the financial impacts of any negotiation items brought up during the presentation of the Finance Plan that will have to be negotiated during the Implementation Phase of The Launch Sequence.

Next, we move into the Implementation phase in earnest. Our Project Financing Checklist™ is the perfect tool for transitioning between planning and putting those plans into practice. We list every important element of the plan in an organic, living document, which helps us keep track of every task that needs to be completed, triple-checked, or avoided at all costs.

Using the considerations listed in the Project Financing Checklist, we then load up the Development Agreement with favorable financing language, making sure to include all financing methods using clear, simple language. If there are any grounds for confusion, it can cause delays, huge profit loss, and major headaches for everyone involved.

At the same time, we are establishing the special district in precise alignment with the Development Agreement. This involves a carefully curated Special District application, which ties together with all the other documents to tell a story. We at Launch are committed to telling that story in such a way that all the pieces of the project are well-connected, coherent, and consistent.

We stay on top of forward progress by holding consistent meetings and identifying roles and responsibilities. Along the way, we ensure our assessment methodology is sound by matching our calculations with reality. This is the heart of implementation: we check and check again that everything is going according to plan, and any deviation is dealt with quickly and effectively. Even a small hitch can derail the entire plan, so attention to detail is absolutely critical.

The Launch Reimbursement System helps track all important costs as we are completing the official statement. If you follow the steps of the Implementation Process, you will be well-equipped to create clear, concise, thoughtful documents that anticipate all potential opportunities and challenges that may occur during the development of the project. Even better, you will have included language in the development and financing agreements to anticipate these items so that the parties never need to "open up" and amend the agreements. When this happens, it inevitably costs the developer hundreds of thousands—if not millions—of dollars.

At this point, we have formed the district and issued the first series of bonds. The bond proceeds are now flowing back to the trustee and being held for distribution to the developer. Now, all the consultants leave, and the developer and district staff are left to look at each other and ask, "Now what?"

Since you are reading this book, you probably can guess the answer. It's time to start the Management Process. Let's explore how to manage your master planned community with ease so that the only thing left for you to do is sit back and "Count Your Fortune."

Public Bidding Assistance

The management of finances is no different from every other part of the Launch Sequence in that there are many components to consider. For example, the method for management is going to be determined by what type of district we have established and what state we are working in. For instance, California has many different regulations compared to North Carolina. Florida is different from Texas. Every state and district has its own nuances, and depending upon the enabling statutes that allow us to form special-purpose taxing districts in that state, we may have to follow the state requirements related to public bidding.

Because we are borrowing public money, in some states, we have to let the "public" have the opportunity to bid on these projects. To do so, we put together a public bidding package that we can take to the market with specific construction-related information for the public infrastructure to be financed by the district bond proceeds. Maybe it's a three-mile, four-lane road. We would provide the public with specifications and allow them to bid during a bid opening on a predetermined date. We then award it to the lowest responsible bidder.

Some states don't require that we do public bidding. They only require competitive bidding, meaning we don't have to go to the public. Instead, we can send a bid package to three or four contractors we feel comfortable with, then determine who we would like to work with based on their responses to those bids.

In other states, primarily Nevada and California, we don't have to do anything. We don't have to do competitive bidding or public bidding, but in these states, we need to pay the prevailing wage, which is union wages for public infrastructure to be constructed and financed by district bond proceeds.

As you are considering how best to manage your project, ensure you know what your state requires. We collaborated with a company of highly sophisticated, publicly traded homebuilders on a project in the southwestern mountain region. They were required to publicly bid on the infrastructure. When we were in the process of forming the district for them, we had multiple meetings with the jurisdiction and the agencies that were going to allow the establishment of the special-purpose taxing district.

In this particular state, we were required to follow the state's public bidding process, which means we had to take the bid package and advertise it in a newspaper of general circulation, as well as other web-based publication services set up specifically for this purpose. We specifically had multiple meetings with the city. We explained to the home builder what they had to do to follow the public bidding requirements of the state. We prepared checklists for them. We ran through the checklist with the city and with our client's representatives in the room. We were very, very clear on what they had to do.

In fact, we asked if we could assist the public building. They said no; they claimed to have everything taken care of. Well, long story short, we formed the district. We were about ready to issue bonds. They had already started constructing, and they had let a lot of contracts.

We were tracking all their reimbursements in the Launch Reimbursement System (LRS), so at this point we asked them for their public bidding documents, their notice of publications, the sealed bids that had come in, the certification of bids, and all of the various different types of paperwork required by their particular state as it relates to demonstrating that they publicly bid the infrastructure as outlined in our checklists that we had given our client.

The information that they gave us clearly indicated that they had not publicly bid the infrastructure. They had competitively bid the infrastructure, meaning they did not publish to the broader public that this opportunity existed. The public should have had the chance to bid for the right to build the infrastructure if they had the right qualifications. Because the project was so far along, the client was unwilling to fix the mistake by redoing the bidding process. The mistake cost them $70 million that they would have received had they publicly bid the infrastructure, and had we issued bonds to build that infrastructure pursuant to what we had been discussing with the agencies and the jurisdictions.

In summary, there are several questions to make sure you answer at this point.

- Will you have to open the project for public bidding?

- Can we limit the project to competitive bidding?

- Do we have to pay the prevailing wage? If so, how will this impact our costs?

- How do we establish the ground rules and documentation necessary by both statute and district agreements?

- Can we prove we have followed everything demanded by project-related documents and statutory requirements to ensure that we can construct out-of-bond proceeds and be reimbursed for our advanced costs, if applicable?

There are a lot of nuances. We can plan these transactions and then implement them, but there are many parties at the table. There could be jurisdictional representatives, agency representatives, district representatives, underwriters, bond counsel, disclosure counsel, appraisers, market consultants, trustees, and the list goes on. All of these people have a hand in making sure that the district is formed and, ultimately, that bonds are issued.

As you've hopefully seen from the past two books in this series, we are involved throughout every step of the process, but our involvement particularly stands out when we reach this point. Managing the transaction is one of the most underappreciated segments of the project, so extra direction and attention here are essential for success.

It is more important than ever to ensure we follow the steps required by statute, because it is during the Management Process that we will start to see reimbursements come in (e.g., cash), but only if we do everything properly. For example, we must continue to provide the district with the information required to build and make the quarterly or semi-annual disclosures to the bondholders. If we don't, we could potentially lose our ability to be reimbursed for that infrastructure, which is a critical part of the plan. Or if we don't follow the SEC requirements outlined in the bond indenture and the developer's continuing disclosure obligations and district disclosure obligations, we could potentially be negatively impacted on future bond issuances.

So this is a critical component of the financing. We can plan and document this transaction perfectly, but there is still a risk of losing everything if we don't follow through on everything required in our transactional documents as it pertains to establishing the district.

Another service we provide in relation to public bidding assistance is preparing public bidding manuals for our clients. As a reminder, we can do as much or as little as our clients would like, but this step tends to be extremely helpful for bringing clarity and direction.

The public bidding manuals follow the three types of bidding that most developer contractors can do in the public realm. The first type is called a design-bid-build, in which we prepare the drawings when they are at a sufficient completion percentage, whether it's thirty, sixty, or ninety percent. It all depends on how much risk the developer wants to take. We bid on those plans, and once the contracts are awarded, we build them.

Another type is the design-build. In this case, we're not looking for the lowest responsible bidder. Instead, we are looking for the most qualified contractor who can design something specific and build it. Often, we see this with specialty wastewater or water treatment plants. In those cases, the jurisdiction describes a specific requirement for the plan, and we put out a request for qualifications from firms that might be able to build according to the specifications.

The third type is a construction manager (CM) at risk, where again, we are not necessarily looking at a bid amount. Instead, we look for qualifications for the CM at risk. Once we have found the best CM, we negotiate the price, and if needed, move to the second contractor on the list, and so on.

You might be wondering why we take the time to prepare bidding manuals for what sound like straightforward situations. We have found that if we're working on a project that may have a ten- to fifty-year life, a lot of project managers are going to come and go during that time. Manuals that accompany the project protect all the work we have done for the duration of the project. Once we have documented the process that the jurisdiction and the district have bought off on, we want to educate our client staff so that every further action is seamless. A new project manager should have to do nothing more than plug and play, meaning they have the appropriate checklists and documents, and they can simply type their inputs, and they are automatically merged into public notices and client contracts.

We try to leave nothing to chance. If a project manager leaves, they aren't taking his or her knowledge of the transaction with them, leaving us to start from scratch. Once we have a successful prototype, we rinse and repeat with a manual that is specific to the project and the client.

Remember, when you get to this step in any project, the developer and the builder need to understand the requirements pursuant to the documents entered into via the development agreement, the district establishment, the district financing agreements, the state legislation, and the enabling acts. That way, all parties do their part to ensure the developer is reimbursed for the infrastructure for which they have advanced funds or which they are building out of bond proceeds.

Takeaway: Ensure you know what your state requires when it comes to public or competitive bidding and follow all steps required by statute.

Track Reimbursable Costs through The Launch Reimbursement System™ (LRS)

After we have done the public bidding, we can start to construct all of our facilities. It is absolutely crucial that everything is documented. If anything slips through the cracks, it is a huge paper chase that no one should have to endure.

Of course, you only need proof that you publicly bid on the facilities if public bidding is required by the state, but at a bare minimum, you need to be tracking all contracts and all change orders as they are processed. All draws and invoices that are eligible for reimbursement through the district should be documented as they are paid. Even the check each invoice is paid with must be easily identifiable in order to prove there was actually a payment. Typically, that's done through some sort of cancelled check or proof of funds transfer.

In our projects, we also get conditional lien releases as a part of those draw requests or invoice payments, then once the project is completed, we ensure we get unconditional lien releases as well. At that point, with the project completed, all punch list items satisfied, and the infrastructure accepted by the jurisdiction, we would need to get acceptance letters. We need to get the as-builts as well.

To help this process along, we implement the Launch Reimbursement System™ (LRS), our proprietary, robust, cloud-based database, which tracks all of this information.

The LRS database contains all the required documents that are necessary pursuant to state-enabling legislation on a project-by-project, state-by-state basis. Because it has all the information, the system reminds us if we are missing any documents or information. For instance, if public bidding is required, we have to put up a notice of bids, bid postings, and publications. If we don't have one of those items, the LRS will flag the project with a notice that we did not upload the posting related to the public bidding of the given facility. We can then make sure to get that from the client. It essentially ensures that we don't overlook any documentation that might hinder the project later.

We typically upload this information on a monthly or quarterly basis. If that sounds like a lot of work, it can be. There is a lot of paperwork, and you have to really dig in to keep up with it. But don't get overwhelmed. We have been doing this for over forty years. We can assist you directly, set up processes for you, or upload documents from your accounting and contracting departments into the LRS.

The LRS is the heavy lifter when it comes to tracking information and identifying what is missing. For example, say we are working on a project in a state that requires us to go out and publish that we are taking bids. If, for some reason, we don't have a bid posting on the property or we have not shown that we have gone to the local newspaper to notify the public of the upcoming bid, then the LRS will remind us. That way, we're not getting two to three years down the road and all of a sudden need to start looking for a notice of publication among all the other files we've collected along the way. The LRS can track all of that for you.

To start you off, here is a short list of the documentation the LRS will prompt you for.

- Notice of bids
- Bid postings
- Publications of up-and-coming bids
- Pre-bid meetings
- Pre-bid meeting notes
- Certifications of bids that have been received
- Award of contract
- Contracts
- Notice to proceed

As it relates to accounting, the LRS tracks:

- Invoices
- Draws
- Change orders

- Certified payrolls
- Proof of payments
- Conditional lien releases
- Acceptance letters
- Bills of sale
- As-built engineer plans

This is not an exhaustive list, but it does provide a head start on the most critical components to be tracked. Then, when we prepare our reimbursement request, which is really just a summary of the information contained in the LRS that is used to get our district engineer certificate, everything we've submitted is eligible for reimbursement. It's all done within the confines of our robust database.

Remember, getting the district is only the start. If you do not have the documentation, don't follow the statutory legislation and district requirements, or otherwise can't submit the documents, you will not be reimbursed.

We always put backup plans in our district agreements using "Plan A" and "Plan B" language in case something goes wrong with the documentation, but it's always best for the documentation to be there in the first place. If there is no paperwork, there is no money.

Takeaway: Utilize the Launch Reimbursement System to track reimbursable costs on a project-by-project basis.

Monitor the Status of All Company Special District Activity through The Launch Control System™

f you are not partnering with us to track your project, it's still critical that your company has some sort of tools on a project-by-project basis so that you know what your contracts are, what you've built to date, and how much has been processed via reimbursement. You also need some indication as to when the next reimbursement will be coming into your project's cash flow.

Whether you have one project or ten, keeping track of everything is a paper jungle. Often, when our clients first get their district, we tell them, "Congratulations, you have a district!" Then, in our very next breath, we say, "Our condolences, you have a district. Now start thinking about documentation retention."

Once we start working for developers and managing their reimbursement process using the LRS, we provide monthly or sometimes weekly analyses on how we are tracking and processing their reimbursements.

In fact, we have a number of clients who have multiple districts in different states, and they're using the districts as a way to control and manage cash flow. Because of the extent of these projects, it is difficult to summarize the status of all districts for all projects across the entire United States. Over the course of the project, updates are necessary, and clarifying questions will often arise.

- What did we estimate would be eligible costs for reimbursement?

- What did we anticipate that we would be generating over time in terms of net proceeds?

- Where are we in the process?

- What have we constructed so far?

- How many bonds have been issued?

- How much has been reimbursed?

- Where are we in the processing of reimbursements?

For us to be able to provide clear analyses for each district, we developed the Launch Control System™, which is a summarization of all of the various LRS projects.

Some of these clients have multiple projects in Texas, some in Arizona, Colorado, or California, and all of these have separate reimbursement systems tracking the reimbursement for that specific project. We use the LRS as a tool to manage each project, but the Launch Control System is an overarching management system. It gives us insight into broader specifications, such as:

- How much money have we spent to date?
- How much money has been processed in the LRS?
- How many reimbursement binders do we have out for approval and reimbursement by the agencies?
- What have we been paid to date?
- What are we short?
- How much money is sitting in the coffers that we haven't yet collected?

It's a crucial system for managing these issues and for enabling us to provide weekly, monthly, and quarterly updates. It could also be an early indication of project challenges. If the system reports have you suddenly asking questions like:

- "How come we're over budget on this project?"
- "Why are we getting so many change orders?"
- "Why aren't reimbursements getting processed?"

The Launch Control System will hold you accountable and get you asking the right questions so that you identify and resolve issues early. All of this is important for keeping all projects moving forward smoothly.

The other reason it is so important to utilize tools like the LRS and Launch Control System is that people in the development industry come and go. And when they go, they take with them a lot of industry knowledge, project-specific information, or district infrastructure financing details. By having all the information in the hands of Launch, you can be confident that we're tracking it for you, and we have institutional knowledge that will never leave with an individual. More importantly, it follows Dan Sullivan's Who Not How® framework. You don't need to know how to do it all. We will be your "who," and we'll take care of the "how" for you.

Takeaway: Utilize the Launch Control System to track documentation across multiple projects and states.

PART 2

Maximize

Prepare and Process Reimbursement Binders using the LRS

N ow, let's get to the exciting part of the LRS and Launch Control System. At this point, we're saying, "Show me the money," and the LRS complies. Once we complete a project, all the documentation is collated in huge binders and ultimately submitted to the district advisors. They will go through and, in essence, audit the documentation to determine that all of the requirements of the public procurement process have been followed. For example, if we had to pay prevailing wage, which is required primarily in the states of California and Nevada, we would have the certified payroll indicating that union wages had been paid on that project.

Our canceled checks, contracts, lien releases, as-builts, and everything else are included in these binders and submitted to the district for what amounts to an audit.

The LRS produces these binders at the press of a couple of buttons. It quantifies everything, describes all the infrastructure, and compiles all the invoices, all the draws, all the lien releases, all the proofs of payment, and every other necessary document into an electronic binder. These things can be thousands of pages long. It all depends on how the plans were drawn up, how the infrastructure was contracted, how it was bid on, and how it was paid for.

Regardless of the project structure and the length of the document, we're able to roll it all up, summarize it, and transmit it electronically to the district engineers for their review. Once we finish putting the binders together through the LRS, we put them on the shelf. That way, when it comes time to issue bonds, we can have everything easily accessible to reference. We'll look at what we're getting reimbursed for through each bond issuance, what we may be charging interest on, what property has been paid for, what real property hasn't been paid for, and more.

This is a specific listing of every piece of infrastructure by invoice or by draw that is eligible for reimbursement. Once we submit these things, then go issue additional bonds, our goal is to get the trustees to release those checks to us without delay or fuss. We will have already proved how much infrastructure has been financed, so there shouldn't be any time lost. The money can go into the project account on day one and go right back out on day two because we already know exactly what we're getting reimbursed for.

Most of the time, we will be processing our reimbursement of costs on a first-in, first-out basis. The primary reason is that it's easiest to track that way. In my opinion, it's also wisest to do it that way. Should there ever be a downturn in the economy, or something similar to what happened in the Great Recession, where no more infrastructure is getting built and no bonds are issued, we might have a lot of infrastructure already in the ground. Well, that infrastructure is going to age, and at some point, the district engineers or financial advisors are going to come in and say, "This infrastructure is too old to reimburse. The remaining life of the infrastructure is shorter than the bond term." For example, if they claim the remaining life of the infrastructure is only ten years, they aren't going to agree to finance it with a twenty-five-year bond.

We've gotten into this conversation a million times with financial advisors, and most of the time, they don't know what they're talking about. That is, they don't know what the useful life of any given infrastructure is. They've heard it somewhere and then try to throw it out as ineligible for reimbursement. But we can go in and show on an invoice-by-invoice basis, using standard engineering practices, that the useful life is much longer than they predicted. We can show that, based on when it was put in service, it has x amount of years left compared to the average life of our bonds. We can therefore make sure we get reimbursed for every cent of eligible infrastructure our clients have put in the ground.

The other beautiful thing about having everything in the LRS is that we don't necessarily have to bother our client every minute of the day. Instead, when it is time to issue another bond, we can have all the information already prepared. We'll lay out the anticipated terms of the new bond, as well as the exact amounts that have been reimbursed to date based on our first-in, first-out method. We'll show them the exact infrastructure that will be the subject of the bond issuance, and all we need from the client is a simple approval.

That's the extent of the involvement we need from them to keep things moving. We get the bond issued and wire the funds back to the client. Of course, they still have to handle making representations related to the bond issuance, signing rep letters, and reviewing those documents, but everything related to the critical path of reimbursing infrastructure, we've got it handled.

When the client doesn't have to worry about the details, they can spend less time worrying about whether they have a lien release for a particular contract and more of their time focusing on the things that make them money. Doesn't that sound ideal?

Takeaway: Prepare reimbursement binders using the LRS, then process reimbursement costs on a first-in, first-out basis.

Perform Developer Continuing Disclosure Obligation

As part of every bond transaction, the SEC requires that the developer report back to the bond buyers regularly. These reports, provided on a quarterly or biannual basis, will form an important part of your bond documents. Through an electronic medium we call EMMA, the developer reports the status of the financing, and whether any material events occurred as defined in the continuing disclosure obligation that the bond buyers should be aware of and concerned about.

The purpose of the Continuing Disclosure Obligation is to give the bond buyers some indication of whether the project is on track as it was described to them when they purchased the bonds. They were provided with an official statement outlining their ability to purchase bonds, and these new reports contain very similar information to that which was initially included in the official statement.

Often, it will call out details and updates relevant to the state of the project. For example, it will generally include where the developer is in the construction process, what the current budget is, how much has been constructed to date, and how much remains to be financed. It may also include a report on how many builders are involved in the project, or whether we have sold any more lots to builders. We would then also include what the builders sold to homeowners over the quarter or six-month period.

Other material events to include in the report include bankruptcy, failure to pay property taxes, or failure to pay debt service related to the bonds. All this does is give the bond buyers an early warning about potential problems with the financing. Or if everything looks normal, the bond buyers can rest assured that the project is proceeding as originally intended.

The Continuing Disclosure Obligation is crucial because if it is not published, it's a bad look for the developer. If they are not forthcoming with the information and making timely reports, the failure is noted in the electronic publication. It could then be taken into consideration for future bond issuances, costing a higher interest rate. This is an unnecessary consequence we never want our clients to face. To prevent forgetfulness or neglect, we often handle these reports on their behalf. We become hassle machines when it comes to making sure this gets done, because we know how critical it is to the financing.

This obligation typically continues until the developer drops below certain acreage requirements. In some instances, if we have a master developer that had sold a big chunk of land to a home builder, then the home builder would step into the shoes of the developer and thus handle reports to the bond buyers. However, regardless of who is responsible, someone on the team or the developer's staff needs to understand what is required and what needs to be done in the event of certain events affecting the sale of land.

As I mentioned before, the other important task we always stay on top of for our clients is accelerating cash into the pro forma. While our developer clients are out building infrastructure, negotiating with jurisdictions, hiring contractors, and working with home builders to sell land, we are always watching the overall progress of the infrastructure to see how fast we are burning through lots and when we may need to open up new phases.

We're working with our clients on a monthly basis, but more importantly, we're handling the major milestones, such as:

- When should we be considering issuing more special assessment bonds to open up a new phase of development?

- Has our assessed valuation contained within the boundaries of the district increased sufficiently to allow us to issue another series of G.O. bonds?

- Are we receiving development impact fee credits for the public infrastructure constructed by the district and included within the jurisdiction's impact fee program?

Everything Launch does is intended to make the Management Process easier for the developer client. Our job is to accelerate cash into the pro forma, and that's what we're doing. If Launch is not working with your organization to do this, then you really need to have a person on staff whose sole responsibility is to do this. They're going to bring huge returns back to the organization through the timely submission of future bond issuances, allowing you to recognize providers to get you the return of cash for infrastructure that's been put into the ground, which you can then utilize to build the next phase of infrastructure.

Takeaway: Never forget to post the Continuing Disclosure Obligation reports.

Perform The Lookback Diagnostic Reviews™ Related to Unreimbursed Construction Costs

The next step is called the Lookback Diagnostic Review. If that sounds like nonsense to you right now, let me explain. Because we have been involved in transactions for over thirty years in some instances, Launch is a repository of knowledge for all the various reimbursement mechanisms that are going to be flowing back to the developer through a specific program. We've been involved in all of the following and more:

- Client job costing reports
- Pre-annexation and development agreements

- Development agreements
- Special district financing agreements
- Financing agreements
- Bond Indentures
- Establishment of reimbursement agreements
- Determination of impact fee credits

During the build-up to the Great Recession, when builders and developers were running as fast as they could to put lots on the ground, we talked to project managers we were working with, and asked, "The city owes you two million dollars for that line extension. Should we go ask them for the money?"

The project managers tell us not to, because they were afraid the city's involvement would slow down their plans and/or approvals. They wanted to just worry about the money later. But after the recession hit, project managers like these were laid off, and the industry came to a grinding halt. Later, even though almost everyone involved in these projects was laid off, we were still around with knowledge of the transactions, so we asked the VP of Land, the President, and the CEO about the two million dollars. Their response was to absolutely get that money and also to see what other money was still out there.

That's what the Lookback Diagnostic Review is all about. It's a unique process we have developed to make sure our clients are being fully reimbursed for every piece of eligible infrastructure on every agreement they have, related to every project.

Having a number of CPAs, auditors, attorneys, and contract administrators on our staff, it is easy to go into the historical records of projects and their agreements. From there, we can determine what reimbursements should have been received, what the remainder is, and who we need to talk to to receive that remainder. This includes everything related to special districts, as we make sure we receive every nickel where appropriate. It could be development impact fees that come back to us, or development impact fee credits that we are owed to the extent that we funded the infrastructure in question.

As part of the Lookback Diagnostic Review, we go through all the reimbursement agreements we may have with the jurisdiction or utility providers, both public and private. We do the same for line extension agreements, cost-sharing agreements, and joint venture agreements. We look at property tax increment agreements to ensure they were calculated properly so we receive our money. The same thing goes for the transaction privilege tax we're supposed to receive, be it construction, retail, or whatever the revenue source is. We will make sure to be reimbursed for all of it.

During this process for the project I mentioned before, we looked at thirty-three companies. Some of these were divisions of public builders, some were divisions of regional builders, and some were private land developers. All told, we found $133 million that the developers were owed by all those companies. Our clients call it manna from heaven. After we perform the Lookback Review, they start receiving these checks with no idea why they are coming in all of a sudden.

We found that because there was such a huge turnaround in organizations during the lead-up to the Great Recession, people were moving from project to project at the speed of sound. Entitlement documents weren't being properly communicated to operations, accounting, or finance departments, so a lot of information was dropped. Situations like this necessitate performing a Lookback Diagnostic of some sort. You can do it yourself, or we can do it for you, but the most important thing you can do is to set up processes to make sure you're recouping all your reimbursements from any and every source.

Whatever type of special district you're working on, make sure you have a process or a system to track all the reimbursements. That way, if there is a loss of personnel, either due to layoffs, attrition, or if those people simply move on to other opportunities, the organization has institutionalized the process to retain all information. When you review that information on a regular basis, you make sure you are not leaving cash on the table. In fact, you're going through all the couch cushions and collecting all the dimes and pennies, which add up to dollars, which, as we have seen, can amount to hundreds of millions of dollars once all is collected.

It takes discipline and rigor to ensure you are receiving all the reimbursements you're owed, but this is the part that makes it all worthwhile.

Takeaway: Institutionalize a process like the Lookback Diagnostic Review to ensure that no reimbursements get lost.

PART 3

Maintain

As Appropriate, Manage the District for the Landowner or Developer

Now you have it all. All the tools you could need for your next master planned community. There's one last item to discuss, and this is something optional that we don't advertise very often. In very specific situations, the jurisdiction in which the district is located might not have experience in administering the district, or it might be a developer controlled district. If they don't know anything about public meeting law, taking minutes, or preparing a budget, we can help. All the details, like getting a tax rate to the county assessor and billing special assessments, can be difficult.

We can set up and manage all of that for the client. We typically only work for developer districts where the developer is in control, but if we form a district and no one knows how to run it, then what good have we done? So in certain instances, we will manage the district for our client. We can make sure bonds get issued, payments are received, and the money all goes back to the trustees to pay back the bondholders.

The list of services we typically get into for our clients is long, but when we're managing the district for them, the list is exhaustive. Once the district has been established, we will work with the board. Typically, the board consists of private members who have been appointed by the jurisdiction ex officio, or it might be land owners within the boundaries of the district, typically the developers. Either way, we will set up the board by approving a president, a secretary, and all the other various titles of the board that are required pursuant to the enabling legislation.

We then work with the district to prepare an annual budget based on a number of factors, including:

- What type of infrastructure will be financed
- What taxes and assessments have to be collected
- What the debt service payments are
- What infrastructure will be acquired
- What maintenance of the district administration function will require

After establishing the budget, we also aid in creating notices for public meetings, we prepare agenda packages and post those to a website, and we go ahead and set up that website for the district. The website needs to have all the required information you would typically see on any other type of jurisdictional website, including budgets, contact information, and meeting minutes. In some instances, we are recording meetings and posting the full recordings to the web, but the requirement varies by state and district. Whatever is needed, we make sure it gets done.

If it seems like a lot to remember, that's because it is. Remember what we say to every client? "Congratulations, you got yourself a special purpose taxing district and you're able to finance $79 million worth of infrastructure." And in the very next breath, we're saying, "Our condolences, you have a small city and now you have to administer it."

What we're offering in this final step is the option to make it all go away. We can be your "who" to make everything happen and make sure it's being done right. Remember, we have no mixed loyalties, so we work strictly for the developer and never for the jurisdiction. When we establish these districts, we manage them via a separate entity. We also always obtain conflict waivers from the district and developer, but really, all we do as part of the district administration is enact what the board assigns to us. It's all administrative; it has nothing to do with decision-making.

One thing is for sure: we didn't get into this business to manage districts. But it's a necessary evil, and more than that, we know how much work it takes. If we can ease the burden on our clients so they experience the kind of success they envisioned, we're all in. We will do whatever it takes for our clients to be able to accomplish their goals of financing infrastructure, reducing costs, and mitigating risk, all with the purpose of enhancing project profitability and returns.

Once our clients are no longer responsible for the district and they've turned it over to the landowners residing within the boundaries of the district, we also relinquish our role and turn it over. Launch is a third-party administrator, but because of our deep knowledge of the district, we can set up even this final transfer of responsibility in such a way as to support ongoing success. As your guide to the Launch Sequence, we have planned the district, implemented the plan through various legal documents, including pre-annexation and development agreements and reimbursement and acquisition agreements, issued the bonds, and everything else that follows. We are well-equipped to administer the district and answer any questions that the governing board or landowners ask in a succinct and knowledgeable manner.

Takeaway: If there is no one else to administer the district, Launch can be your "who."

Next Steps

We've made it to the very end of the Management Process and the Launch Sequence itself. If you have stuck with it this far, you are well prepared to take the next steps toward your master planned community.

Most of our clients are very involved and focused during the planning and implementation of their district, but when it comes to the Management Process, their attention wanes. Remember, following through on those plans for the long term is crucial. We can have the best plan and implementation, but if we don't manage everything properly and follow all requirements, we will lose our ability to be reimbursed for everything we have financed through the district. Period. End of story.

I have seen it happen time after time where people don't maintain the proper records, they don't follow the public procurement codes, they don't publicly bid (if required), or make any other seemingly small mistakes, and they end up with no reimbursements.

In conclusion, pay close attention to the management of your districts, either through training your team well on thoughtful processes or hiring somebody like Launch to help you and your team collect every nickel you are entitled to.

This is where the rubber hits the road. Without this stage of the Launch Sequence, you will not be reimbursed. That's how critical it is. Stay focused and attentive; dot your i's and cross your t's. You have the tools you need, as long as you follow the Management Process through to the end.

Afterword

As you have learned more about how the Management Process works, we hope you feel inspired to take advantage of the simplicity and clarity of The Launch Sequence. Maybe you see echoes of your own master planned community dreams in these pages of success stories.

Most likely, though, your set of dangers, opportunities, and strengths is different from anything you've heard about here. That is even more exciting! Every project is unique, and we would love to come up with new ways to leverage your D.O.S. and help you implement your plans.

Regardless of where you are in your project, Launch is ready for you.

Scan the QR Code below to Access
Supplemental Documents and
Book Bonuses

About the Author

Carter is an author and the Managing Principal of Launch Development Finance Advisors. Prior to the founding of Launch, Carter was the Co-Founder and Managing Principal of Development Planning and Financing Group. Preceding this, Carter was a Manager in the real estate consulting department of the national accounting firm of Kenneth Leventhal & Company in both the Phoenix, Arizona, and Newport Beach, California offices. Carter is a Certified

Public Accountant in Arizona, California, and Texas, as well as a former State Certified Real Estate Appraiser in Arizona. He holds a master's degree in Real Estate Development from the University of Southern California and a bachelor's degree in Business Economics from the University of California, Santa Barbara.

With over forty years of experience in the real estate consulting industry, Carter's area of specialty is in the formulation and implementation of land-secured financings for large-scale developments and the formulation of development strategies for large-scale master-planned communities.

Carter served as a City of Phoenix's Camelback Village Planning Committee member. He is a full member of the Urban Land Institute and Valley Partnership, and he is a member of numerous Building Industry Associations in Arizona, California, Idaho, and Texas. Carter authored the 2008 and 2016 National Association of Home Builders' Impact Fee Handbook as well as the 2025 Impact Fee Update.

LAUNCH®
DEVELOPMENT FINANCE ADVISORS

OUR SERVICES

Launch is a transaction-based real estate consulting firm that specializes in the financing of public infrastructure that serves our clients' development projects.

- Land Secured Financing
- The Launch Bond®
- Development Impact Fees
- Entitlement Analysis
- Cash Flow Analysis
- Development & Financing Agreement Negotiations
- Legislative Initiatives
- District Management
- Litigation Support
- Fiscal Impact Studies
- Public Bidding & Reimbursement Services

LAUNCH-DFA.COM

THIS BOOK IS PROTECTED INTELLECTUAL PROPERTY

Instant IP [IP]

The author of this book values Intellectual Property. The book you just read is protected by Instant IP[IP], a proprietary process, which integrates blockchain technology giving Intellectual Property "Global Protection." By creating a "Time-Stamped" smart contract that can never be tampered with or changed, we establish "First Use" that tracks back to the author.

Instant IP [IP] functions much like a Pre-Patent since it provides an immutable "First Use" of the Intellectual Property. This is achieved through our proprietary process of leveraging blockchain technology and smart contracts. As a result, proving "First Use" is simple through a global and verifiable smart contract. By protecting intellectual property with blockchain technology and smart contracts, we establish a "First to File" event.

Protected by Instant IP [IP]

LEARN MORE AT INSTANTIP.TODAY